About the Author

Rona Octavia was brought up in Swansea and has South American heritage on her mother's side.

Rona is the youngest of five girls and is very passionate about sports, nature, painting, music and writing.

Dedication

This book is dedicated to my parents and family.

I am thankful for their never-ending love and support.

I am forever grateful to my Pa for his storytelling and
my Mumma for her encouragement in all I do.

Rona Octavia

KNOCK ME DOWN AND WATCH ME COME BACK STRONGER

AUSTIN MACAULEY
PUBLISHERS LTD.

A CIP catalogue record for this title is available from the British Library.

ISBN 9781785542800 (Paperback)
ISBN 9781785542817 (Hardback)
ISBN 9781785542824 (E-Book)

www.austinmacauley.com

First Published (2016)
Austin Macauley Publishers Ltd.
25 Canada Square
Canary Wharf
London
E14 5LQ

Acknowledgments

I gratefully acknowledge the support I received from Uncle Mike, Uncle Ralph, Isaac, Poppy and Lucinda and for their strength and humour on this journey we shared.

"Nothing so frightens me as writing but nothing so satisfies me. It is like a swimmer in the (English) Channel; you face the stingrays and waves and cold and grease, and finally you reach the other shore, and you put your foot on the ground – aaaahhhh!"

Maya Angelou, 1989.

Chapter 1

The Discovery

Where do you start when someone that you have let all your barriers down for, betray you? She had been weird for months, her mood swings, her twisted morality, her general personality had changed. We had no social life at all - at least not as a couple. She didn't even bother with her friends and when I mentioned to her that we should to do something together, she would go mad, cleaning an already very tidy, ultra-clean house and would then complain that I never cleaned! I remember talking to a colleague about all the strange goings on and weird outbursts. She told me it sounded like my girlfriend may be seeing someone else. I remember saying "Nah, she wouldn't do that, she never tells lies!"

It was January 3rd and I was driving home from work. It was 8am and the traffic was heavy. The rain bounced relentlessly off my car. On the drive home, my colleague's words haunted me. I remember praying to God, "Please don't let it be true."

I had moved out for an agreed month, which had turned into two because we kept meeting and dating even though we were going to try and be on a break for a month.

Arguments haunted my head. Suspicious behaviour came into my mind. She was always texting, then stopping whenever I went near her. Constantly on the laptop, then closing it when I went into the room she was in – all so strange, looking for arguments when no normal person would act in such a way.

That morning I climbed wearily up my stairs and slowly got into bed, thoughts running in my mind, jumbling into my worst fears. How can I find out if she is cheating? It hit me! I knew her so well. I jumped out of bed. I guessed her password on her email account. I opened her email and looked. Nothing suspicious was there. Thank goodness! Another horrible thought hit me. She had three email accounts. I hacked into her second one and there it was! Dating back from the 26th November the previous year. Sex emails, flirty emails, innuendos aplenty – all to one woman!! I felt sick. My hands started trembling, my body shivered in conjunction with all this. All the time she was looking to pick arguments but still claiming to love me and want me!! What a load of bullshit! F…..g a…...e! Why did I move all the way from Wales to be with someone who made my life so miserable? Blackburn truly did resemble blackness to me. How was I to find a way out? I printed out all the emails, as shaking, crying, quivering, I woke up my housemates with my stuttering and crying. On hearing me, they came to me quietly, waiting, then tried to settle me with sweet tea, hardly knowing me. At the time, I had not long moved into the house we now shared. Issy held me tight and let me cry my heart out in her arms.

How does a lost soul find its way back from a broken heart and become a person again? After much crying on the telephone to my parents, who were in Portugal that month, I put the phone down and I looked in the mirror. My eyes were blood shot. I saw a fat five foot five woman staring at me. I looked old and haggard. Hardly someone you would want to say hello to on the street, never mind commit to. I said out loud... "Rona Octavia. Look at yourself. You are a loser!"

I sat down in a daze, looking for a distraction. I happened upon a newspaper advert for the RNLI and suddenly an old dream flashed into my memory – the dream to swim the English Channel; so in shock and feeling sick, I looked it up and within half an hour, I had signed up to swim. I just needed to find myself a pilot to help me cross the sea to France. You need a pilot boat to be beside you, to sign you in from the English coast and sign you out from the French coast. This is for safety reasons but also because you need an official on the boat to ensure the swimmer has followed all the guidelines set by the Channel Swimming Society and no cheating has taken place. The Channel Swimming secretary told me that I would have a very slim chance as they are booked up for two years normally. I wasn't going to let this deter me so I rang all the pilots and, true to what the swim secretary said, they were all booked up. My last call was to a Peter Reed. To my surprise, he had a slot for the 23rd September! This is funny because I had emailed the secretary saying I wanted to swim on the 23rd. I took it as providence: that it was meant to be, so Peter got the ball rolling.

I got up and wiped my eyes and I stood in front of the mirror once again and tried to smile. It just made me look pathetic. I spoke to myself again in my lunacy. I tried to find a positive angle while my heart physically pained me. I said to myself. "This time next year you will be proud and happy. You may have lost everything but you can get it all back again." I felt disgusted with myself. How had I let myself go?

Chapter Two

The Road to Recovery

I suppose any ordinary person would actually train to their fittest level and then book up to swim the Channel when they were comfortable. I am no ordinary person – my Pa brought me up to think that there was no such word as "can't". As a youngster my Mumma and my Pa spent a great deal of time and love ferrying me to all my sports. They were like a taxi service all during the week and on weekends, for galas and competitions. My Granny was a woman who believed that if you put your mind to a task, you must see it through. So this was my secret steel; positivity was to be my shield and sword – or at least this was the plan!

I didn't really know how to function at first. I can understand why people write of heartbreak and put it to music. Finally, I understood the love poems that we had read at school and, as an adult, I tried to empathize with. My first few days were impossible. I was unable to sleep for nightmares or waking up in cold sweats or worse still, waking up, thinking she was next to me, holding me. She may as well have taken a knife to me, stabbed me and bashed me a thousand times. I was a shadow of who I was meant to be.

So how do you combat nightmares and no sleep? Well, I ditched my car, bought waterproofs and began just going out on my bike and cycling for hours and hours nonstop. I didn't know Manchester and had no idea where I was going. It was a bitter winter so I bought gloves, two pairs, and wore them on top of each other. I would spend hours just crying while cycling not knowing where I was or what I was doing.

I was short on money so the first time the tyre on my bicycle had a puncture, it was a nightmare - I did not know what to do. Luckily for me, Salford is a cheerful and friendly place. I asked two men that were passing. "Sorry to disturb you but how exactly do you repair a puncture on a bicycle?" They were such nice guys; they went through it all step by step for me and showed me how to fix my tyre. I think they may have been construction workers as some new houses were being built not too far from where I lived. To explain where I lived then, I can only tell you it is like something from Coronation Street; curtains twitch on a daily basis and everyone is always on the streets chatting away. I felt this tenderness in my heart for a strange supposedly, rough place. For me it was peaceful, calm and full of characters.

On account of having her haunt my soul on a daily basis, I had to stay out of the house when Issy and Roz, my housemates, were not home, because, alone, I would only sleep or cry, or worse still, wonder why the hell I was even alive.

It was while I was at my lowest I had the real discovery of who I was and where I came from. My family rallied around me. My parents Ronald and Claudette have a holiday home in the Algarve and they are of retirement age and that is where they were when I found out about the cheating. I telephoned them in tears and after speaking to them, my Mumma got in touch with Aunty Betto and Uncle and told them of my situation as they could not get a flight home straight away. They drove to be with me from the Cotswolds within a moment's notice. They are my Godparents and I have always seen them as my second parents. They were always there when I was growing up. Their children Venita and Paul, my cousins, are more like a brother and a sister. I will never forget how my Aunty held me just like my Mumma would. I spent such an amount of time crying, she calmed me and glued me back together. My Uncle Mike was calm and in control. They both took me out for food and well, I couldn't eat but to be with them was like having my Mumma and Pa with me.

I found it hard to concentrate, so much so that when I opened a book I would read maybe five words and then I would feel sick and well, I would cry. So in the evenings when not at work, I would put on a cheery face and either go to work or sit with my housemates.

I had always been quite a shy person socially, always a little paranoid of what people thought of me. I worried that I may talk too much or stutter if I said something at all. It was crippling for me but sitting with Issy and Roz, filled me with such calmness and a real easiness, it made my soul scream less painfully. You know, as an adult time really flies. As a child, a day seemed like five for me. Well on account of being unable to sleep, my days seemed like years, maybe centuries in fact. I took on more shifts to escape the real world. I didn't want to be left alone with my thoughts. My work face was easy. It was a distraction. At work I needed no cuddles, I wanted no home cooking (I had taken joy in cooking for her). I didn't rattle around in my house turning over the past. The love I craved was just a little cut that I managed to stem while working.

I planned my days where I finished work at 8am so that I would cycle to the gym, have coffee, toast and jam. I still took pleasure in coffee; it made me smile for an immeasurable amount of time. I got into the habit of finding things to be grateful for, so each morning I would give thanks for my health, a roof over my head, my family and good coffee. It helped me drag my mind from negativity and into the positive thought process.

Just before reality would hit me, I would drag myself like a zombie – slowly and surely, for an ice cold shower. I would not allow sleep to take me over, because I would only dream of her if I put my head down. I would go into the swimming pool where I was a gym member and I would swim. Oh my goodness! How I would swim! I would just swim and swim and I would go into a deep meditation... 1, 2, 3 breathe to the right. 1, 2, 3 breathe to the left. At first, due to being fat and unfit, I had to stop after ten lengths. After a while, I found my brain could control the pain and exhaustion my body felt and so I began just swimming and swimming in an altered state of mind. I then found, when it was really difficult, old songs sprang to my mind. Songs that made me smile from my childhood.

"Take me down
To the paradise city
Where the grass is green
And the girls are pretty "
(Guns and Roses)

"Wild thing, I think I love you
But I wanna know for sure
Come on, hold me tight, I love you"
(The Troggs)

I am the youngest of five sisters – there is eighteen years between my eldest sister and me so I have always been the baby of the family. Memories of my four older sisters sunning themselves on our parents' roof made me smile. The old ghetto blaster, blasting out Whitney Houston, Michael Jackson, David Bowie, Adam Ant…

It was strange because all the therapy in the world would not have helped but being submerged in water and keeping my mind to happy thoughts, brought something else to me. I became serene inside. The anger, pain and hurt that crushed my very existence melted away into nostalgic memories of my beautiful family and the unconditional love they have always immersed me in since birth.

My Granny was such a character – she had a Guyanese accent and a strong faith and religion that kept me amused as a child but as an adult, it grounded me. I found myself remembering funny stories of my Granny and how she was still a fiery Guyanese woman, even when she appeared to be a frail, old lady. The funny thing was, my thoughts in the water made everything seem like it was present day, not past. This one shopping trip I went on with my two cousins Venita and Paul stuck in my mind. I would like to share with you how it came into my mind. We were quite young and shopping with our Granny in Ealing, London. I have to tell you about the incident as it played on my mind…

"Boy, why you in my way!" The little old lady shouted in a fiery tone. She sucks her teeth at the young man. He was minding his own business, shopping for baked beans. The poor student gets the back of his legs whacked with a crooked walking stick. "OOOOeee!" He yelps in pain and jumps out of her way. I go bright red and temporarily camouflage behind the little trolley she wheels around the market like a weapon of mass destruction. The young man's yelp attracts the whole aisle in our direction.

Granny's hair is curly and black – she wears a smart coat, plaid.

Her other weapon is her handbag, hanging menacingly from her arm. She is small and if you were to see her, you would think she was just an innocent old lady. I know better. Her curls always tighten up and form small horns just before she does something embarrassing. But, on the sly, I quite like my Granny's antics. It makes shopping so much more interesting.

Granny is examining her shopping item by item, checking the prices, making sure she is not being overcharged. I pity anyone that crosses Granny's path. Venita, Paul and I argue about who can stand furthest back; we do this silently so Granny doesn't notice as she always has one of us holding her arm. After assisting Granny and letting her hold our arm, we end up walking lopsided for a week if we are picked. I think she may see us as a battering ram.

It is incredible, even when someone has passed on, how the memory of that person can still make everything seem so real, so present. This is just one of the memories that surfaced in my mind and cheered me up.

I had given myself just nine months to train for my Channel swim. From what I had read, most people give themselves two years to be ready for the swim. I was fourteen stone and none of my clothes truly fitted me and I had become too scared to socialize. The thought of meeting my friends or new people scared me massively. To make matters worse, I had moved into a house that I shared with two girls that I didn't even know. I suppose life has to throw you into situations for you to realise who your really are. My Mumma spoke to me once when I was at the lowest that I had ever been. I was in a pit of real despair.

She told me "Sometimes Rowie, we have to reach our lowest point to find out who we truly are." It took a while for this to settle in to my mind.

I had been stuck in a loop; in my mind there was nothing left to live for. Sometimes when you reach a deep depression like I did, you become so self absorbed that (and it is a cycle where nothing and nobody can help you) you become selfish, never intentionally, it just comes over you. What my Mumma said to me stuck in my mind because it was true. I had reached the lowest of the low and I suddenly started to realise who I was. It dawned on me. I had lost my identity. I had become a rat; a fat rat in a sewer, racing nowhere but in my mind. When I was "living", I thought it was something good. I realised I was wasting my life, working all the time, never truly living. I never saw my family because I had work. I couldn't maintain close friendships because I had work. Blackburn, the place I couldn't settle in, the place where I couldn't make friends, became like an old friend; ironically I started to settle there even though I didn't live there anymore.

I had an old bike that I had bought from an amazing recycle bicycle shop in Swansea. The guy, called Ian, who ran it always had world music and reggae music playing and talked in a laidback, chilled way. I had found a bike in a tip (I was very short of money at the time) and exchanged it for a bike in his shop – it cost me just ten pounds.

Some days after work, instead of taking my bike on the train, I would cycle home instead. When I was not working, I would cycle. At first it killed me, I would cycle on the flat and then walk up any hill in my path. I found a lovely route of cycling to Manchester. I would cycle through Blackburn, Darwen, the West Pennine Moors and then Bolton through to Swinton ending up in Salford. It was whilst cycling this route that I realised how beautiful Lancashire was. I suddenly opened my eyes to the quaint old red houses, to the gorgeous stone houses, then all the mature trees lining my route, amazing hills of lush grass and wild flowers. I found that my eyes began to hunger for the country and my soul craved to be near nature. I made it my routine to stop and have my breakfast in a field on the top of the Moors. I got in the habit of taking my pocket rocket and I would brew fresh coffee in the open field. I would just sit down and breathe in the country air. I would listen to the silence that gradually became alive with sounds of birds singing and other noises that lulled me into a perfect peace.

Due to it being winter, the sun always rose when I was over the West Pennine Moors so, sometimes, I would just lie down on the dewy morning grass and watch the sunrise. It made me smile to be close to nature and the elements; I found that no matter what the weather, I always craved to be outside. I wanted to observe life but at the same time be with nature.

My shyness gently ebbed away. I started to cycle with a grin on my face, saying good morning and smiling to people who I passed on my way. What I found lovely was that people who were walking my way responded with huge grins and smiles and passing cyclists with nods.

Chapter Three

Salford

Life in Salford was interesting too. Issy and Ros really took me in as a friend. We would chat and watch TV together and Issy would cook for us. At first I struggled to eat in front of them because of my shyness but not very long after, I didn't mind at all. I have to admit I was slightly in awe of the girls as they both looked like models. Ros had studied jewellery making at University and Issy had studied fashion and when they dressed up, my goodness everyone's heads turned. The best thing was, they didn't realise how pretty they were. They involved me in such an easy way that the panic attacks I used to get, didn't exist anymore. Every night before we went out, we would document the evening by taking pictures. I still hated pictures of myself so I would take photos of them. It was like a whole new world had opened up for me being with them. They took me out to the Northern Quarter in Manchester and, well like I said, they were so good looking that when we went out, we all had our drinks bought for us. I had never really gone to straight places previously – all the people I was friendly with were gay, so for me it was so fresh and exciting. They took me to amazing places with good music and incredible atmosphere on a regular basis. How could I have forgotten how easy life could be? The mornings were my favourite.

Sometimes we would all be in at the same time and Issy would make us bacon sarnies and the best cup of tea ever! It was strange, I had lost the love of my life but in a weird twist of fate, a whole new world had opened up to me. Once I had let Issy and Ros into my life, it was like I had become an open book. All the time I had believed that the only person I needed was myself and that nobody liked me, this was really a type of paranoia I had developed – it began to disappear, my barriers were dropping.

My very good friend from London came up to visit me one weekend and we went out together. I had always known Lisa to be quite shy. One evening, after a good meal and going to a few bars, I bet her three drinks that she wouldn't sing at a karaoke bar. Lisa grinned at me and, to my surprise said. "Right, Rowie, we are on!" She downed her red wine. We were on Canal Street so she confidently approached the drag queen and put her name down to sing. Well, we drank and danced and before we knew it, they called on Lisa to sing. Lisa prodded me. "Remember Rowie, you owe me three drinks of my choice."

Well I nearly fainted. Lisa sang an amazing rendition of "Just Another Manic Monday" by the Bangles. She was awesome! So after loads of applause and people approaching her to say how good she was, I asked her what her drink choices were. Lisa being Lisa, chose wine. In fact, she downed the three glasses of red wine very quickly. She later told me that she had been practicing that song and it was her favourite to sing out. I smiled to myself; Lisa was a dark horse.

When we moved on to out next bar, the cold night air hit her and she seemed fine but when we went on to our next club Lisa became almost zombie-like. She had recently got married to a girl she met in London so, in between me giving her copious amounts of water, she was on a settee, texting her love to her wife. Lisa has a really strong personality and any mention of "Let's go home" was rebuffed to "Naaah ROWIE, we shall party!" So after maybe the tenth glass of water I fetched from the bar, three girls approached me thinking I was on my own. I explained I was with my mate from London but she was just resting after downing three glasses of wine she won from a bet. Denise was very smiley and had shoulder length hair with blue eyes. I learnt she was out with her best mate Jackie and Jackie's girlfriend Lucy. Within five minutes they were downing shots and making me do the same. Lisa luckily started to come back down to earth. I would have loved to know what drunken texts she had sent to her wife and if they were readable. So we moved to another club and danced all night. I found myself dancing like nobody was watching me and, for the first time in my adult life, I felt really free. Lisa was the life and soul of the party and I found that she helped me to be relaxed. Like I said earlier, when you open up your life to good things, more good things come in.

From that night on, I became good friends with Denise, Jackie and Lucy. I was invited out quite a lot with this newfound group of friends. It's funny, all the time of complaining I didn't have friends up North, I had created a self-fulfilling prophecy. I had been putting up so many barriers and finding so many reasons why people wouldn't like me, I realised it was just me disliking myself.

I had kept my ambitions of swimming the Channel to myself whilst I was training so when I woke up in the mornings, I would cycle laps around Salford and Manchester.

Chapter 4

My Research Into Previous Channel Swims

My research into past Channel swims led me to realize that there was a slight problem and this was the reason why a lot of people fail to get across the Channel. It was that they had hypothermia from the cold water when they were exposed to it for a long time. Well, given the fact that it was now the month of February, and me living nowhere near the sea, and the factor that it was far too cold to swim in any lakes or, travel home to Wales to go swimming in the sea (as there were no lifeguards during the winter months), I found my solution was to run myself cold baths and acclimatize to the coldness that way. The first cold bath I had was like what I would imagine hell to be like but in reverse. At first I jumped out of the bath. Next I hyperventilated. Due to the cold weather, I also contracted a nasty chest infection which put my training back to just cycling.

When I hyperventilated it reminded me of one particular occasion when I was in Acton, London, going to Church with my Granny and Paul my cousin. My Granny went to Church on a regular basis and was a senior in the Pentecostal Church in London. One Sunday, we arrived to a very good service where the congregation was singing and dancing. Paul and I were always amused that the people that went to church there always sang passionately but out of tune. So we would bet each other on who could do the worst yet convincing singing and dancing. About halfway through the service this particular day, I felt a little unwell so went to the bathroom. I was about eleven so I was just getting used to having periods. When I came back from the toilet and tried to get back into my seat, I felt quite unwell again. Unfortunately for me, this was at the point of the service when the Holy Spirit would come and talk in tongues to the worshippers. So when I felt faint and unwell, the congregation got very excited and suddenly many hands were placed on my body and face and people started praying for me. Of course I didn't get better so the congregation decided to carry me outside on a chair. Many shouted "God! Bless this child! She has been taken over by evil spirits. We must exorcise her to save her soul!!" At this point, somebody shoved smelling salts up my nose and many others placed their hands all over my body and tried to exorcise the evil spirits out of me. Of course because I wasn't well and also scared, I started to hyperventilate.

Paul, my cousin, shouted "Shouldn't we get an ambulance?" The worshippers shouted in their Caribbean and London accents. "No, Jesus will save her!" "God take these evil spirits from this child!" This was all now taking place on the pavement outside the Church with about forty worshippers. Paul snuck off and phoned the ambulance accompanied by my Granny.

The ambulance came and I was carried into it and treated for hyperventilation. The paramedics looked out of the window of the ambulance and I remember one of them saying, "Blimey, no wonder you hyperventilated. They are all holding on the ambulance and shouting for the evil spirits to leave."

My Granny took me home and I was put to rest. For the remainder of that week, different churchgoers came to pray with me and preach the word of God to me. On the positive side, I was treated with many biscuits and chocolates.

I continued researching other people's stories of how they failed to cross the Channel. I thought I could learn from other people's mistakes. I had one real problem that could halt any chances to swim the Channel. I needed to be in full health for my swim in September and at this time in February, I was on citalopram, an anti-depressant.

You see when you put all your eggs into one basket and become head over heels in love with someone, you can lose sight of your own individuality and forget about your dreams and passions. This is something I did and of course a natural conclusion was that when the relationship broke down, I felt like a nuclear bomb had destroyed my whole world. My mistake was I had also not been able to form any friendships whilst living in Blackburn. My whole world was her and her family. I had become rather suicidal at the time of our relationship breakdown and the doctor had placed me on anti-depressants; this is something I needed to come off if my dream of swimming the Channel was to be realised.

It is strange how you can have years of being stuck in a rut and then suddenly when you hit rock bottom and you think it's all over, you realise how much people care and love you. I knew in February I was not yet strong enough to have my full medical so I looked into ways I could beat depression. My heart felt crushed every single day on waking up but I discovered that I had to keep busy doing things I really liked. As such, I took up painting again. The painting helped my insomnia because if I did manage to sleep, I would dream of her. Or, when I woke in confusion, I thought I was in the flat that she and I once shared. Just so

I would be able to sleep, I thought that if I kept myself busy, my conscious self would be exhausted as well as my body and mind. I painted most nights and wrote all my feelings down to expel them from my mind.

At one point, I had about twenty paintings on canvas in my tiny room. I cycled to a local art café and gave the owner all my paintings. I explained that he could have them and sell them for what he wanted and in return, I would like coffee and breakfast now and again. He sold them all and at a time when I was very broke. On the days I ate in his café, I observed the world outside, lost in daydreams of swimming the Channel.

I bought all the music I loved and had it on nonstop, day and night. I wrote goal lists for the day. At first, it included getting up at a certain time, showering and other basic things like getting food from the shops. You see when you are depressed, the temptation is to just curl up and sleep and not even shower. So my goal lists worked day by day, with times of when I was going to do things. I had a very bad memory – they say that you get this too when you are depressed. My mind still could not even concentrate on a single book. I would start to read a sentence only to find my mind was not taking a single thing in. How do you combat that? You cannot do that with a list, that's for sure. For me, it was a slower process. Each day I did try to read but each day, I put the same book down and got no further than possibly a page.

My family and friends called me every day. My Mumma and Pa emailed me every single day from Portugal and rang me when they could. Weeks became months. Quite quickly, I found that ditching my car and cycling everywhere improved my being, especially the early bike rides when the world still seemed to be asleep. I felt almost reconnected to nature. I used my bike so much that I went through quite a few inner tubes with all the punctures and actually broke the chain guard. I stupidly didn't realise this until I ripped my third pair of trousers. So I dug out my old wellies that I had bought for Glastonbury a few years back, and had not used since. I found they kept me lovely and dry and also were extremely comfortable, although I guess I looked funny, cycling like a farmer girl round Manchester and Blackburn.

The cold baths became more bearable after a while and then I was able to submerge myself for over an hour and I noticed that if I slowed down my breathing and sang a good song in my head, I actually felt warm. So this was a very good thing to remember.

I have a best mate who lives in Australia and is a nurse. I sought her advice about coming off my anti-depressants. She told me that it takes a while to do so and that the doctor weans you off with lower dosages. This was to be my downfall in a way as it could take months to be weaned off and it was late March. I needed a full medical to be sent off to The Channel Swimming Association by May. I stupidly went cold turkey. I woke up one day and decided that today would be the day. I hated the reliance I had on the tablets and I naively thought I would be okay. As it turned out, I felt sick quite a lot and became really dizzy. I ignored the side effects and struggled on for a while; it made training very difficult. Of course it would have been far easier to just take the tablets – but I was focusing on my larger goal of swimming the Channel so I dealt with it. When withdrawals symptoms were a bit difficult, I slept with the help of a small amount of whiskey. (I don't recommend this to anyone).

Thankfully, I got through it. I found it hard to sleep anyway so I just kept on with my work and as soon as I finished my night shift, I would fit an hour in the gym to strengthen my shoulders and then four hours in the pool. At first, I worked blindly in the gym unsure of what to do to strengthen my arms. This was very important because from my research on failed attempts, many people give up because they had shoulder injuries. I had already prepared myself for hypothermia but I was very aware that my shoulders needed to be a lot stronger if they were to take the strain. I had read it takes 150,000 strokes to get across the English Channel. I was very lucky that a really nice gym instructor questioned me on what I was training for. I told him sheepishly, that I was training to swim the English Channel. He was such a nice man; he would spend ages giving me tips, telling me what to read, eat and even tried out smoothies on me. I worked on his advice at the gym and found in turn, my performance in the pool improved greatly.

Chapter Five

Start of my Training

As the weather became warmer I would jump on the train and take myself for bike rides in the Lake District. The closeness to nature and its beauty made me very happy and, no matter how difficult the cycle ride, I enjoyed it.

When May came, I went outdoor swimming in the Salford Quays. My first swim was daunting – I was the shortest, chubbiest swimmer queuing up to go in the Quay. We had to queue to pay, so I chatted to a few people and when they heard that I intended to swim the English Channel in September, I could see doubt mist over their eyes and then stories of failed attempts by their mates came into the conversation. These people were all like Greek Gods and Goddesses in my eyes. Their bodies were so muscled and toned it, made me blush. One swimmer pointed out a guy to me and I was told that he was about eighty. His body was muscular and strong looking - I was amazed. I had no idea outdoor swimming was so popular. I had turned up half an hour early but still had to wait as they only let a certain number of swimmers in. To my disappointment for health and safety reasons, they would only let you swim if you had a wetsuit on. The Channel Swimming Association only recognizes swims with no wetsuits. For my Channel swim I was only allowed an ordinary swimming costume.

I hired a wetsuit that day and it was so strange to go into water with little dinghies that had lifeguards in and maybe fifty swimmers, bobbing up and down. I was advised to just jump into the water but when I did so, to my horror, the icy cold water put my body into shock. I guess because I was all toasty and warm from my bike ride before and then submerging my body into icy cold water, I just put my body into shock. Well you can guess what happened; my heart felt like it was going to burst from my chest and I felt like it was going extremely fast and my breathing went bad so that I couldn't swim. The lifeguards came near me on the boats to help; my pride stopped me from getting out. I put my thumbs up and floated on my back for a little bit. I then noticed a couple swimming together as I had swum to some railings to acclimatize. I asked if I could join them and they were so friendly, they said yes. So I swam with them, matching their pace and after a few minutes, my body was just fine. I slowed down my breathing and concentrated on singing in my head to bring myself back into control. I enjoyed the swim and almost the comradeship that the swimmers displayed for each other – it was a lovely feeling, another world unfolding before me. I disliked swimming in the wetsuit as all my movements seemed restricted but over time I got used to it.

I found that my fear of socializing and dancing, heck, even singing, disappearing. I had taken singing lessons to improve my confidence the autumn before. I went to London to visit my mate Lisa in March. I had a new lease of life where I had a thirst for being around people. I felt like my old self once again. I was inquisitive and almost happy.

I had been cycling around Manchester daily so I thought nothing about taking my bike on the train to London. In my naive enthusiasm, I thought that London would be easier by bike and I could find my way round quite quickly. Hmmm…. this was not the case; the rugby was on. Lisa being Welsh, was watching it in a pub near London Bridge and I had agreed to meet her there. I got off the train at Euston and asked for directions to London Bridge. I spoke to many taxi drivers and people from abroad, who were very friendly and pointed me this way and that. But with London having so many one way streets, I got totally lost.

I stopped at a road and saw a bright yellow bike approaching my direction and I shouted. "Excuse me!" To my surprise, a lady stopped and I asked if she knew the way to London Bridge. This lady was so kind, she just said "Follow me" and basically cycled with me all the way to my route. All I had to do was follow her. ` We chatted at traffic lights and I discovered she was an animator from Hong Kong. It also happened that she lived nowhere near London Bridge and in fact, lived in the opposite direction. I was in awe of this woman. She had just finished work, tired but willing to take me to my route even though it was miles out of her way! I kept in contact with Lexi and she turned out to be a great person to know. Her online statuses are always positive and she has recommended a few good books for me to read relating to sports.

On finally reaching Lisa, she took me and some of her friends to an event in Brick Lane and we saw a number of really good bands. One band stood out because the female singer came on stage wearing all black and sunglasses when it was pitch black. The next thing we knew, she whipped off her clothes to reveal corset, suspenders, stocking and stilettos. She had real balls to do that. She was very pretty and it was clear that the crowd loved her. She sang Katy Perry's "I kissed a girl" from a lesbian's point of view. I had not heard a woman sing like that live, and, not care about her sexuality. I found it empowering. I carried on dancing with my friends when the DJ sets started. Later that evening, I found out that the lady who sang on stage turned out to be a lady I was chatting to earlier. I had suffered a displacement and didn't make the connection. We swapped contact details and from that night, I kept in touch with Lucinda and she became a strong and positive influence for me. I found out that she was a project manager by day. She was the front woman for her band and wrote all the music in the night times. Lucinda also managed her band members. Later, I saw that she was a very good cook and would make all her meals from scratch and in addition, had an amazing social life. We spent many an evening chatting away and I found a great friend in Lucinda. She taught me the beauty of time management – this, she explained to me was how she fitted so much into her life. Lucinda was brought up in Germany and her mother is from the Philippines and her father was German. Our conversations revolved around positivity and our dream goals and also stories about her dating - I always found that amusing as she was on a quest for a girl who could only be described as "Miss World". Lucinda also gave me a lot of advice on nutrition and how to organize myself better. It's strange how sometimes the love of your life can disappear and exit from your life but in turn, many inspiring and beautiful people can enter your life. I won't pretend my heart was healed. In fact, I still cried most days but it seemed like things were falling into place with my life.

Chapter Six

My Fitness Level

My training included some nights of not sleeping very well, so I would cycle to Blackburn at half past four in the mornings. These cycling days were very special to me. Whenever I approached a hill, in my mind I would shout "Eaaaasseeey! Eaassssseeeey." I found chanting positive affirmations helped me get over hard tasks like massive hills.

Some days I would get lost and cycle my way over to Burnley and found that Rawtenstall was almost like Wales with its great hills and wildlife. Those hills really took me by surprise; they had the perfect windy bends that would trick me into thinking I was almost done, so just as I relaxed, another massive hill would approach. With the weather being warmer, I cycled most days in flip-flops and loved how the air rushed against my feet.

I made more friends; well, when I say more, in reality they were already wanting to hang out with me but because I didn't see myself as interesting when I first moved to Blackburn, I never took them up on their invites. Cass, I had known when I first moved up to Blackburn but I never took her up on her invites to hang out. She got in contact with me again and I found we had many things in common. Cass and I would spend quite a lot of time together and she would also meet me for swims. She is so positive and smiley; I found my spirits lifted just by being in her company for a few minutes. Karina is another friend who I had known but never accepted her offers to hang out. She is a keen cyclist and has since taken me on many brilliant cycle routes in Blackburn. I had lived there for four years but never realized how special or beautiful it was until I started going on these long rides on my own and with Karina.

I decided to take up bouldering to strengthen my shoulders so I started going on my own. One day I found myself chatting to my friend Jed about it and he just said "Oh I love climbing; I will come along." It was brilliant when we decided to go climbing and Cass and Karina came too and we would spend many rainy evenings bouldering away. One afternoon, it was just Jed and I bouldering, I found myself a little scared of getting to the highest parts of the walls and was coaxed up by Jed. "Go on Rowie! Go on!" So I got pretty high and then just froze. It brought back a memory of a seven year old Rona climbing a wall at school and freezing, like a picture swaying on a wall. The teachers had to come and rescue me because I was dangling off a massive drop with no hope of getting back up or down. I had climbed it as a dare. Jed shouted "Rowie! Rowie jump!" I did jump and landed flat on my face on some matting. Apparently it didn't look like a jump it was more of a slither and then a splat.

I had used my £10 bike so much and racked up so many miles that I hadn't realized how important it was to service bikes. I remember one ride home back to Manchester from Blackburn. I was very proud of myself for getting to the West Pennine Moors without getting off and walking up hills so, as I got to the top of the hill, I really powered myself down the hill to maximize my speed. I suddenly saw a big pothole and jammed my brakes on, only to realize they were not working and this pothole was getting a lot closer and because it was a rainy day, if I swerved around it I may have lost control of my bike.

I jammed my wellies in the wheel bit and stopped myself that way. The wellies worked very well as brakes but I had caused them to have a hole in, so the rest of my ride was quite a soggy one home.

From that day, I learnt that I needed to pay more attention to the condition of my bike and look after it more so it could look after me. Luckily for me, a lovely man at work who somehow knew I was broke, left me new brake pads in an envelope and later on, he even fitted them for me.

I found that wherever I was, people would rally round to help me if I found myself in an awkward or difficult situation. Some days, when I was late for my train, I would sprint up the stairs at Manchester, Victoria with my bike on my shoulder. Often the conductor would delay the trains slightly for me and not let it leave the platform until I was safely on the train. Some days I was so tired from all of my training, I would fall into a very deep sleep on the train and find myself either jumping off too soon and cycling miles home or not waking up until the train was going to the train yard. Once, I managed to get myself trapped on the train just as it was leaving for the yard. There was another time where I had slept my entire journey, only to find myself on the train going back to where it came from. Whenever I got myself in these strange situations, there was always someone to help me or direct me to where I needed to be. My days always turned out to be really quite special.

I eventually managed to pass a full medical test and had lost quite a bit of weight as well. Instead of being fat, my intense training had left me leaner and more toned. After one night-shift, I was cycling really quite fast to the train station and it happened almost in slow motion. I saw a car driving into me. I managed to swerve just enough but found he still made impact with my front wheel and my leg. I also hit my head on the floor when falling. I have always had a habit of jumping up very fast whenever I get injured and laughing it off. I did just that. He was very concerned about hitting me but I told him I was fine. He had not checked his exit before coming out of a side street and drove into my left side. It was a taxi that hit me. As I walked to the train station, I felt quite sick and realised that my leg was really sore. When I went home I realized that I had what can only be described as slight concussion. My bike had a front wheel buckle and some damage so I had to find £60 to get myself back on the road. I was lucky. Issy took good care of me those few days and my leg was just a bit bruised – I had swerved in enough time so that the damage wasn't severe. I was very lucky that day because if a car was behind me, I would have probably been critically injured.

Of course my parents were not told of this but my friends who lived locally knew about it as well as my best friend Lucinda, from London. Lucinda had not heard from me for a few days after she had heard about the accident, so she texted my mumma who was home in Swansea at the time and asked her where I was. And, was I recovering after the accident?

My Mumma who had also been trying to get in touch with me, was shocked and upset to hear of the accident and, when she was finally able to make contact with me, she questioned me about all the safety aspects of cycling. She was annoyed to hear I had been in hospital and not informed her. I told her that I did not want to worry her and pa. My father emailed me from Portugal asking me about back lights for bike, helmet, etc., and I assured him I had everything in place.

A couple of months later, another car did the same thing to me but in Manchester this time. A lady hadn't looked at her blind spot. I had dropped my bike that time but again knocked my head. I saw this as a sign to wear a bike helmet and saved up for a good helmet to keep myself safe. I made sure I kept up with my training and if my bike was being fixed, I got myself running or in the gym as well as swimming.

My fear of interacting with people had vanished by June. I found that the weather meant I could get my camping gear out so when it was dry and warm, I got the train up to the Lake District and got off near Burton in Kendal. It was a gorgeous sunny day so I cycled all the way to Lake Windermere with all my camping gear on my back. I have to admit I had no idea where I was going but I just decided I would see where the day took me. I experienced quite a few punctures as I cycled around. I stopped at a Little Chef at one point as I was so hungry from cycling and decided to eat apple pie and custard which is my favourite dessert.

My parents and I always used to stop at a Little Chef on our journeys to London to visit my Granny and Uncle John and Aunty Gem and our various other relatives in London, as well as the trips to the Cotswolds to see my Godparents Aunty Betto and Uncle Mike. I found myself reminiscing about those long road journeys. Whenever my Pa thought I was asleep, he would deliberately wake me up and tell me to look at the scenery. I smiled to myself because now as an adult I appreciated the picturesque scenery and clung on to the memories of those long car journeys that were always two hours more than they should have been because my Pa knew of a short cut. In reality, he just wanted us all to have an adventure and I think he must have had his own agenda because we would always end up getting lost somewhere exciting.

Chapter 7

Lake Windermere

When I got near to Lake Windermere, I stopped at an outdoors' shop, which was like a cave with all sorts of treasures. I asked the shop owner where I could camp for the night and I explained to him that I wanted a spot where I could swim this evening and first thing in the morning. This guy told me of a number of spots and must have seen my eyes glaze over. I explained to him that I wanted to be nearer to where the locals went and away from tourists. The shop owner was a real hippy laid-back type of guy, lean with muscle and wise with age. He told me where the locals went and advised me to only put my tent up when the sun went down otherwise I would get moved on. I thanked him so much for his advice and I have to admit I felt like hugging him. I get this feeling sometimes in life when I meet someone. I find people give different vibes and his was very sweet and kind natured.

I got on my bike and I cycled to the start of a forest as directed. I then dismounted from my bike and carried it through different uneven bits of ground that needed climbing through in parts. As I descended into the beautiful forest, I found the sun shone through the trees and the younger me emerged for a few moments and stories of fairies that my Pa used to tell me and my sisters came into my mind and made me smile.

When I got through to the edge of the forest, that's when I saw the water and the jetty. It was like I had found my private haven. I tied my bike to a tree and found somewhere to hide my rucksack. I got changed into my swimming costume and I have to admit thoughts of the Loch Ness monster and the Jaws' theme tune came to mind as I swam up and down my little bit of lake. I had decided not to drift from my spot but just to swim near the forest so the land was always in sight.

My goodness, the water soothed my body, I relaxed and felt the tiredness from cycling all day easing away. The coolness of the water made my brain rush and my heart sing. I felt like I was in paradise. After my swim, I took my bike and left all my camping gear well-hidden and cycled to a shop and bought myself some food to cook on my pocket rocket camping gas stove. I also bought some ginger beer and water. I cooked some "cook-up rice" (Guyanese expression for rice, vegetables and everything thrown in) on a massive rock that acted like a table top for me and I then sat at the edge of the jetty, ate my dinner and had my cool ginger beer watching the sunset. I observed the swans and ducks skimming over the rippling water after flight. Due to the sun setting, the light reflected amazing colours into the water. It rippled with pinks, reds, yellows and purples, it made me truly appreciate how wonderful life is when you strip it back to just nature and the simple things.

When it was dark, I put on my headlamp, erected my tent and for a little while, after it was set up, it became my home for the night - it was cosy. I then watched the moon and the stars and tried to remember the different constellations I was shown as a child. When it got chilly, I snuggled up in my sleeping bag and slept. I was aware of being on my own on the edge of a forest so I slept with my penknife and spanner, for my bike, near to me. Now and again I woke up from hearing noises of what I assumed to be birds or maybe the wind causing splashes in the water. It was only when it was dark and silent, I remembered that one of my few fears in life is that of darkness. However, the moonlight was like a massive night light for me that night. Luckily, I went into a deep sleep from the exhausting day I had experienced.

I set my alarm for 6am and I rose with the sun. I tidied up and put my tent away and made myself porridge, brewed real coffee and observed nature, whilst listening to all that was surrounding me; the breeze through the trees, the birds singing, swans swimming and landing on the water and ducks playing. Every now and again, I could see the bubbles from fish that had surfaced and I found that my soul felt at peace. I read at the edge of the jetty and watched the world and when the sun reached a high point in the sky, I swam again and felt refreshed from just being outdoors.

When the day got warmer, I changed and went for a walk through the forest and around the lake for the rest of the day. I visited the lakes whenever I had time off work and stayed when I could – it was such a nice way to train.

Chapter 8

Telling My Family About My Channel Swim

July came quickly and I found myself scarily close to September. It was at a family party at Aunty Betto and Uncle Mike's in the Cotswolds that I told my family about my intention to swim the English Channel. It was greeted with shock and disbelief and too many questions I could not answer. I was also faced with a lot of doubt and support – it was a strange mix that made my head spin. You see my Mumma had spent most of the year flying back and forth to see me from Portugal and well, I had been secretive with my plans of the Channel swim and the training I was doing. So she was maybe my biggest critic and did not want to hear of the subject. She told me that I should not attempt it and the money I had paid the boatman already could have gone to my past debts.

I have to say I was very upset by the lack of support I seemed to face. However, my Aunty Lynette who lives in Italy, on saying goodbye to me, on her return home after the party the next day, said "Rowie I know you can do it. Good luck my love."

It made me stronger and more determined to swim when my Mumma said I could not do this challenge because I was not fit enough. You see I am a stubborn creature, if someone says I can't do something, then I strive to do it where sports are concerned.

When I was eleven I was competing in the shot put for my school. I had beaten all the schools and had got to the final stages where I had the chance to compete with my school athletics team to compete against all the schools in Wales. However, a week before the finals, I broke two of my fingers playing rugby and was told that I was not allowed to compete. Well, I wailed and I cried and I nagged my parents every day until they gave me written consent to compete, only after I had seen our doctor to get his approval. I had to plead with my doctor to allow me to compete and I was given a more secure splint to protect my broken fingers. My father had dedicated many mornings at 6am for me to practice my shot putting in our local Singleton park. Now, with having a splint on my hand, the way I threw the shot had to change. Pa spent hours practicing with me and my Mumma spent time watching us. I even practiced in my lunch breaks at school. My headmaster, Mr. Fayne, was an amazing, kindly man who gave me his time to help me. The result was that I won a gold medal on the day of the shot put competition with two broken fingers in a splint.

Picture 1 - Myself

Picture 2 - My bike

Picture 3 - Training on my bike

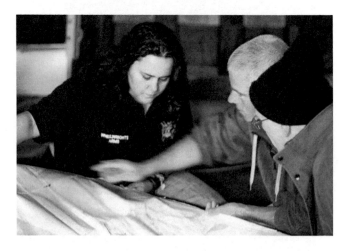

Picture 6 -Peter the boat pilot and his son Peter junior showing me route across channel

Picture 8 – goose fat just applied

Picture 21 - Being watched from the pilot boat

Picture 4 - Caswell Bay, Swansea, practice swim

Picture 27 - My swim and COVER PHOTOGRAPH

*Picture 25 - Dry land - outside my Uncle's pub in Dover.
My crew members and me*

Picture 14 - My feed time

Picture 11 - In the rhythm

Picture 10 - First hour in the sea at dawn

Picture 12 - My swim

Picture 13 - Another photograph from my swim

Picture 5 - RNLI lifeguards in Caswell Bay, Swansea

Picture 9 – Photo call - Just about to dive in

Picture 20 - Rowenna, the pilot boat

Picture 21 - Poppy watching over me

Picture 22 - French soil

Picture 23 - Back on the boat

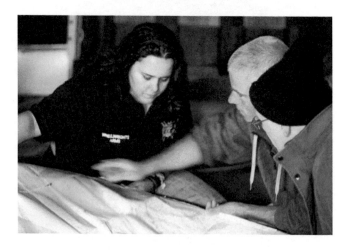

Picture 7 -Looking at map for swim

Picture 19 - Coming up for air after being sick

Picture 16 - just after my feed

Picture 15 - My feed

Picture 17 - mid stroke

Picture 18 - Mumma's favourite picture

Picture 26 - My younger cousins who greeted me after the swim

Chapter Eight

Preparation For The Swim

We had another family party in August as it was my Uncle Ralph's 60th birthday. He told me to swim in his cover outdoor pool so he and everyone could see how I was doing. After my swim for them, my uncle drummed up all his guests to sponsor me and because it was his birthday party, everyone did as he asked. He also spoke to my Mumma and encouraged her to support me. My Mumma felt I had not trained enough to do this challenge so would not be convinced.

I had booked time off for the party and also to spend time with my Mumma and so on the car journey back to Swansea, I spent hours explaining about my Channel swim and told her that no amount of "no" from her would put me off doing it. My Mumma being the feisty South American lady that she is, told me that she needed to see me more organized and I was to show her my plans. I told her that my Uncle Mike had kindly agreed to come on my boat to support me. Like I said before, he is like a second pa to me, and also lived much of his younger days on a boat and in addition, had a passion for building boats. His natural calm and patient persona was also ideal because I realised that I would need very calm people on my team that didn't panic in case I got into difficulty. I chose my cousins Venita and Paul and my niece Poppy. I also chose my cousin Venita's then fiancé, Isaac, to be second in command on the pilot boat, after my Uncle Mike. I explained to my Mumma that I needed to do a qualifying swim at the end of August and would love her to support me with this. My Mumma set about asking me numerous questions and it was only then that I realised I had planned for cold water, cramp, being injured but the one thing I had not prepared for, was where I was going to stay or where any of my supporters would stay before or during my swim.

My Mumma got in contact with my uncle Ralph who owned a pub in Dover and asked him if I could set off from his pub for my swim from Folkestone. My uncle kindly agreed and so in late August, I set about inviting people to support me, telling them that they could stay at my uncle's pub for the duration. I have always been last minute in all that I do. I blame this for being born a week late! As you can imagine, due to work commitments and money issues, many people were unable to commit to coming to Dover at this late stage.

My eldest sister Razia was behind me all the way, texting me and wanting to be a crew member but I knew that like my Mumma and Pa, she would not be able to see me struggling and would be wanting my Uncle Mike to pull me out at the first sign of my struggle. She stayed behind. My third sister Annie had other commitments and couldn't make the journey. I knew that they were with me in spirit and wanted to be informed every step of the way. My fourth sister Merrie had a young baby and could not drive at the time but wanted to be there to support me but it was not possible as Mumma's car was full to overflowing with all my feeds, warm clothing, blankets, etc.

I was secretly pleased with this because I didn't want a crowd of people waiting for me after my swim. That August, a small part of me was scared of failure. I had done a few swims in my home town of Swansea before letting my mum know about my Channel Swim plan.

One swim in the sea really stuck in my memory. It was my first swim, testing how I would manage with the waves over a period of time. I wore a bright yellow Channel swimming hat and my own hat underneath because I had to wear their hat for my swim. The water was still warm so I didn't use goose fat, not just yet as it was still July.

The sea was wild and strong, and the lifeguards had sectioned the beach off, one side for swimmers and one side for surfers. I decided to get in and, at first my fear of the waves made me very cautious; I forgot to tell you I am scared of waves too. A memory came back to me as I jumped up and down like a child testing how the waves would hit me.

I was on holiday with my parents in Tenerife and we went to the seaside every day when my Mumma would pack us picnics and take a magazine to read whilst my father and I would go nearer to the sea and when the waves came in, we would see if we could stand against them without being knocked over. During this one holiday, it became clear why the beach had red flags on it and why my Mumma sometimes call my Pa "Jinx Bond".

The waves looked bigger than a house to me. My Pa was really keen to go in the sea. He said, "Come on Rowie, let's go in." I declined and explained that I thought the red flags meant something and the waves looked too big. My Pa insisted quite a bit, but being sixteen, I had come to that stubborn age of not shifting once I had made my mind up. I lay in the sun with my Mumma and read my book. Pa went into the sea and made it beyond the big waves so he seemed like just a dot to me on the horizon. After about half an hour the dot, which was my Pa, was waving at me quite happily in the sea. I waved back with a big grin and shouted "Hiya pa!" I could hear him shout something back, I think it sounded like "lp" "lp" I disturbed my Mumma. She looked ever so glamorous in the sun. "Mumma. Hey, Pa is waving to us. I think he is calling for something though." My Mumma jumped up. "Rowie your pa is asking for help. Go!!" My Mumma had always taken me swimming ever since I was a baby because she had a fear for water and didn't want to pass it on to me. I had gone swimming all through my life and, as a teenager, achieved my rookie lifeguard qualification just before going on holiday. My Mumma never said no to any sports or activities while my Pa worked away. She would arrange her life around my sports and swims.

My Pa was still waving and shouting what sounded like "'elp", which now sounded a bit, more like "help". I looked at my Mumma and told her I was scared. She looked at me and pointed to the sea "Go Rowie!" I was my Pa's only hope and, a strong swimmer, so it made sense. I went into the shallow part of the sea and a massive wave hit me, knocked me off my feet and tumble tossed me on my face. I got up and, this time when the next big wave came for me, I held my breath and went right under the crest before it could break on me. I did this about five times more before I finally reached my Pa and each time the wave scared me with its anger and height.

My Pa was there in front of me and just as I got to him and I went to put my hands under his arm to bring him back to shore, luckily for me, two massive lifeguards must have seen me foolhardily going into the surf and followed me because when I got to my pa, they were just behind me. Two lifeguards then towed my pa back to shore. I was so relieved because my pa is a bear of a man – he was always built like a massive doorframe.

On that holiday my father managed to show my Mumma and I a fruit from a cactus plant which he said was edible. In his eagerness, I think to impress my Mumma, he grabbed it to bring it back it to us. Soon he was yelping and my Mumma spent maybe over an hour or so, using a tweezer to get all the needles from the cactus fruit out of his hand.

You wouldn't believe it but my pa also managed to snorkel in the sea and a big wave shoved him onto a rock causing him to be cut and bleeding. Yes, I was sent to go and get him again. During this same holiday my pa managed to break his toe on a rock whilst swimming and finally, he got stung by a massive jellyfish and was quite ill and in pain for a few days. We spent many a holiday looking for pharmacist for Pa due to his mishaps. At the age of sixteen, I realized exactly why my pa was called Jinx Bond.

I was brought back to the present day and swimming in Caswell Bay, by a wave that was full of seaweed and I ended up swallowing too much salty water. These childhood memories made me smile and it then gave me the courage to actually start swimming properly in the sea and I remembered what my Mumma always taught me. She always wanted me to brave and not to be scared by things that scared her. She wanted me always to be strong. I became so courageous on this beautiful day in July, I decided to swim right out into the sea. I wanted to swim out, past all the rocks and past all the cliffs that separated me from the big ocean.

In Caswell Bay on the Gower coast, at the time when I was swimming, there was a beautiful family of sea lions that would always come and play with surfers and swimmers. I swam past them. They were playing with a paddle boarder. I felt strong from my mother and father. Suddenly, the ocean became eerie and silent and, parallel to my right, just as I took my breath, a massive grey body with a fin jumped out of the water less than fifty meters away from me. I didn't wait around to see what type of finned creature it was. The cowardy custard came back to me. In total fear, I swam right out of the sea and my belly hit the shallow waters rather ungracefully.

Later I told the lifeguard of what I had seen and he scratched his head. In a fine, deep Welsh voice he said, "Ah, it's probably a basking shark or a porpoise." My face must have been full of fear because he then cleared his throat and said "Oh you know, maybe a dolphin." The idea of it being a dolphin seemed so much nicer so I happily got back in the sea and decided to only swim in the area that was lifeguarded.

My sea swims were interesting because it was only me training then and I found it hard to train myself on how I was to be fed. You see when you swim the Channel, you have to be fed about every half an hour during the swim. The way I practiced being fed was a little eccentric. I asked permission at the gym I used and explained what I was doing so after my gym sessions, I would take a whole variety of foods in with me to test which would work better. I practiced feeding on my back. The foods I tried were blueberries, grapes, bananas, pasta, jelly beans, mars bars, strawberries and cook-up rice. To swim the Channel, you need to have high energy foods to keep your body going but you also need a good amount of carbohydrates. I had read that to get me across the Channel, I would need the equivalent of one hundred and fifty slices of bread. So I had to research what was really needed in great depth, in between my training sessions.

My ex's parents still kept in touch with me and out of love, wanted to remain in my life. I was thankful for this because they had been very sweet to me from the beginning, right through to the end of the relationship. I was invited to their caravan in Morecambe. I went up one afternoon after work and they taught me a card game with their friends and gave me cooked food they had saved for me.

I went for a swim at my gym, which was also in Morecambe and whilst practicing my bizarre feeding techniques and different strokes, a friendly man called Garth stopped me. He asked me if I was a professional swimmer. I told him "No, but I was hoping to swim the English Channel and was training for that." I was asked what I was doing it for. I told him about my family home in Swansea and that each morning I would wake up and on the days my pa was home, he would make me breakfast and tell me stories of Archie Crow. One morning we were up early and the sun was rising, I could see a land beyond the sea from our kitchen window and that's when my pa told me of Captain Webb, the first man who swam across the English Channel.

It stuck in my mind; that beautiful sunrise and wanting to cross the land beyond the sea. My pa said that when he was a boy, he knew of a man who would swim from the Mumbles Pier to Port Talbot every year. Port Talbot is about 7.5 nautical miles or so from Swansea. I had decided I would swim the Channel to raise money for the RNLI who are a charity and lifeguard most of our beaches and each year save many lives. In Swansea, there is a legend of Swansea Jack, a dog that saved many lives in his lifetime. It felt like a cause to support. My Mumma would always take me to the Mumbles Pier for breakfast as a treat when she could afford it. Sometimes we would watch the RNLI boats launch and other times my Mumma would indulge me and take me to the men who were on duty there and let me ask questions on how I could volunteer and do what they were doing. The second cause I chose was RAPID UK. I had a newfound respect for this organization because doctors, nurses and firemen, amongst others, volunteer to go to disaster zones to administer aid through this organization.

After I told Garth my story, he then told me that he was a reporter and would like to follow my swim and write an article for the local newspaper. I explained this would be brilliant because I have left fundraising till the last minute and that I would appreciate any help to raise money for these causes.

Throughout my days of training, I found that many people that I met had something to teach me or were there to help me and I felt my depression lift just from pure love from these kindly souls. My love for my ex's parents, Anne and Dave, remained and I found good friends in them. They rallied their friends to sponsor me and help me raise money for RNLI and RAPID UK.

Whenever I went home to Swansea to train, I always arrived on the train with my bicycle and had a massive rucksack on my back. Without fail, my Mumma would cook me wholesome foods. She would cook curries and other Guyanese Indian delights as well. I could tell she knew I was serious now about wanting to swim the Channel and she would help me organize press releases so that I would raise even more money for my charities. When I was in pain from training too much, she would run me a hot bath and would be my sounding board when I had dilemmas.

One night I decided to go for a run and ran down to Swansea Bay – it was still summer so the sun was just setting. I sat on the beach wall and the memories of my parents, sisters, family and friends flooded my heart. I watched the waves kiss each other and the golden colours set behind the sea. I studied the ocean and it made me feel full of awe; it was so calm as it lapped the sand and I felt a shiver down my back.

Just over a month was left and I was fitter, stronger and my mind was clear and determined but would it be enough for me get across the English Channel? It was a full moon this night and I remembered what the pilot told me. For me to swim the Channel it has to be a neap tide. This meant at the point of a neap tide, the moon has less gravitational pull on the tides. In theory, the waves would be not as strong for me to swim against and I would have more of a chance of success. At this point, I felt at nature's mercy and realized I would need the ocean's kindness to help me through.

I got up and started my jog home; I stopped and let a father and a child pass me on their bikes. The Swansea bay front has a wonderful footpath for cyclists and walkers and more memories came to me. I remembered being younger and chubby, my mother giving me her engagement ring to wear just for an hour or so. We were in Broadstairs in Kent. I was nine. I went to wash my hands in the sea and my Mumma's ring came off. Of course, when my father found out, I was chased some great length of the beach by him. My Mumma was quite embarrassed, willing us not to run toward her, because my father and I were both packing some chubbiness back then and he was yelling at me.

After that holiday, we were both put on a soup diet and each morning of the summer holidays, we would get up at 6am and after breakfasting, etc., we were down the park practicing sports and then my Mumma had us cycle down the waterfront.

My first experience of cycling on a road with my Pa was interesting. It started well but as we got to the main road, my Pa sped off and forgot to tell me how to navigate a roundabout. We cycled on the waterfront and not long after, stopped for an ice cream. My Mumma had no idea of this, of course. We had got into the habit of always stopping for a coffee or ice-cream. Joe's ice-cream is legendary in Swansea and it was our favourite ice-cream haunt.

My Pa even decided to cycle off quite fast on the Swansea bay front and luckily for me, I couldn't keep up. He had gone down a ramp at a tremendous pace and his front wheel hit the sand, at which point he did a somersault and landed on his back with his bike on top of him.

As I ran home I was filled with more laughter as I remembered one weekend my Mumma set us off to Oxwich Bay on our bikes for the exercise and drove to meet us later. It was a good many hours cycling to get there. We had chips and then my Pa was asked to show me how to rock climb. He dutifully took me but decided to take our bikes. I found myself rock climbing with my bike up a massive hill. My father must have been into forest trials when he was younger because he then set off at quite a speed down the mountain. The next thing I heard was "Heeeeeeeeeeelp!" He had managed to hit a tree root and fell off the side of the mountain. I saw my father holding on to some tree roots and rocks. I bent down and started to help him. Luckily some strong cyclists came and helped me take him back onto the path again. It made me grin as I ran home.

My brother- in- law, Andrew, would also take me out cycling when my Pa was away working. He was a daredevil and would teach me all sorts of tricks on my bike, taught me how to play rugby and football. I was lucky to have two brothers in law growing up and Chris would also spend his time showing me tricks on the skateboard and how to do kick ups with the football. My sisters were all very fearless and during my childhood I was always taken on adventures with them. As I ran home, I realized that all those months ago I thought I had nothing left to live for. How could I be so blind to all the love I have had around me since coming into this world?

Chapter Nine

September Has Come

September soon came and I had to do my six-hour qualifying swim. My Mumma was now behind me 100% and was like my trainer. She would tell me when she thought that I wasn't good enough and I would fight back by pushing myself to be better and faster. We went to Caswell Bay that day and I asked my mum to help feed me while I stayed in the ocean for six hours. We made up food and flasks – I had chosen hot chocolate and hot Ribena. I also wanted to test what an energy drink would do to me, so I chose three different varieties. The weather had taken a turn for the worse; I layered myself with goose fat and got in the ocean.

My Mumma has a way of befriending everyone and she explained to the lifeguards what I was doing; they then offered to feed me whilst I was in the sea. She then sat in the café and watched me from a distance. This part I was thankful for because she would have got a chill waiting on the cold wet sand. The lifeguards were brilliant, they were RNLI lifeguards and because the weather was so rough, I was the only swimmer and by myself in the sea. I was told the sea was fourteen degrees centigrade. The lifeguards were true to their word and, at each half an hour, they came into the ocean wearing their wetsuits and gave me my feeds.

The waves didn't scare me anymore. I saw them as friends and ducked under them and at times rode them. I felt like a seal and in my mind, I knew I was mainly made of water and if I relaxed more, then the sea would look after me. I had decided whilst swimming in the sea, I would keep my eyes shut because the encounter with the big finned creature made me realize that actually, I didn't want to know what was in the sea. Sadly for me, I swam into a jellyfish and got stung on my neck. The pain was severe but I knew I could not leave the sea otherwise it would be game over. I told the lifeguard when they came to feed me and I was told the salt water was best for the sting. He seemed a little worried about me and asked me if I would like to leave but I said, "No, I would like to stay in thank you." The hot chocolate was like liquid gold to me. I continued swimming. This is when I met a regular swimmer. His name was Phil and he had been sent into the ocean by my Mumma to check that I was okay. Not sure how, but my mum has a great way of getting things done in the most charming of ways. Phil gave me some great advice. I had been experiencing cramp from testing out energy drinks and I realized this was a reaction from my body. He told me to swim on my back if I ever got cramp. I did this and he swam off after telling me stories of regular sea swimmers that swam the coast of Swansea to Port Talbot. This cheered me up through the pain of cramp and being stung by jellyfish. It meant the story my father told me as a child, must have been true.

I stayed in the ocean and the weather got worse and worse. The sky went grey and thundery; it rained down on me badly and the waves grumbled at me for being in their ocean. I looked into the horizon and could see nothing but grey dark clouds and a lonely ship. The clouds got sliced through with lightening and the thunder roared in the sky like a lion about to charge. I have always been scared of thunder (still am) and found fear take over my body. I sang a happy tune in my head and tried to ignore it.

The lightening grew closer and it hit the sea just beyond the horizon, it then hit the ship. I got called over by the lifeguard and he advised me that if the storm got closer, I would need to leave the sea for my own safety. In his deep Welsh accent he asked. "Are you sure you're ok?" "I am great." I replied. I did not say that was I was freezing and a little fearful. I went off and carried on swimming. I knew I was near my six hours. Just one more hour to go. Fifty minutes passed...

My Mumma came down from the cafe in the pouring rain and shouted at me to get out. Now a Guyanese mother is always right with time and I could set my clock by my Mumma. She beckoned to me and I swam out of the ocean just as the storm calmed. She wrapped me in a towel and gave me hot chocolate. I looked at my watch and I had got out ten minutes too early. My mum had mistakenly called me out too early. (I later found out that my Mumma was actually waving in my direction because she couldn't see me very well and hadn't called me out). I found myself feeling a little sick and dizzy but I didn't want to complain because I knew my Mumma would stop my Channel swim. I got in the car and my Mumma made it very warm for me. At this point I felt colder. When I got home, I had a warm shower but it wasn't warm it was freezing to my skin. At this point I realized I was hypothermic which meant that my body temperature had dropped. I was very ill all night. My Mumma made me soup and while I ate it, I realized my qualifying time was a fail because I had come out too early from the sea. That night I had a feverish sleep and felt my body suffer massively.

When I got up next the morning, I felt awful. It was a huge effort to go back to Caswell but I remembered one of my Mumma's sayings. "You can rest when you are dead." So I had my breakfast, a warm shower and we drove to Caswell Bay. My parents and I have spent many summer holidays in Caswell Bay with my sisters and Granny and later on with my cousins and nieces and nephew. We used to pack picnics and take our blankets and just enjoy the warmth of the sun and the lovely sandy beach where we would frolic in the sea, chasing the smaller waves and attempt rock climbing. I put the goose fat on and got back into the sea. This time, I made sure my drinks were warm, not hot, and I made sure that at no point, I stopped swimming even if I had cramp. I made sure I used my arms and kept swimming and didn't stop. This time the six hour swim was successful. The sea was still wild and the day was still cold but thankfully the lifeguards followed my mum's instructions and being the only person in the sea, they made sure I was well looked after.

It was after I had completed my qualifying swim that I was told that the day before, I had gone quite blue but the lifeguards did not pull me out because I was still active and it was just tinges on my face. The lifeguards advised my mum on what aftercare I needed when exiting cold water. I was to be heated up slowly, with layers, not to heat the car up on the journey home, just keep the car warm. I was only to have warm drinks because any extremes can put me in shock.

I found myself having quite a painful chest after my qualifying swim and realized I had got myself some sort of a chill. I deliberately didn't tell my mum and continued preparing for the Channel Swim.

Chapter Ten

The Journey to my Swim and Final Preparation

My Mumma and I drove to Canterbury to see my sister Robina and family who lived there and was not too far from my uncle's pub from where I would start my journey to the swim. On the journey there, I was questioned about every eventuality. I was to have a radio interview with a local station and this was to be my third interview by radio. Any inhibitions I had before my depression had now vanished. I survived the interview without a stutter and even managed to crack a few jokes. My Mumma was in the ante room where I was being interviewed, on one occasion. One of my sisters, Merrie, who had a young baby at the time and who was listening on the radio from Wales, was texting my Mumma telling her to prompt me every now and again about my charities. She had wanted to come and support me but the car was filled from boot to back seat with all my feeds and warm clothing and blankets, etc. So whenever there was a lull, when the interviewer was playing a record, because it was a music channel, my Mumma would come in, transmit messages from Merrie, have a little chat and then exit.

I went to my Uncle Ralph after the interview and he asked me how I had prepared my team on the boat. At that point, I realized that I hadn't planned anything for my crew. My uncle told me to make a list which every member of my crew should have. We should all have the exact information with my instructions. He told my mum I was like a boxer and she was my promoter as she was helping me to organise everything. I went to my sister's house that night and drafted a "Rowie Manual" It is as follows:

- If my goggles break, there are two pairs on the boat.

- I have a spare cap on the boat.

- If I get stung don't worry, I just need to work through the pain. Please remind me of this.

- I may get cramp in both legs, don't panic, just remind me to keep calm. Float on back till it eases.

- I may get confused, do not worry – possibly bring me in for hot chocolate.

- I don't want to know how far I have gone, do not tell me how many miles I have left.

- Find ways to make me smile if I become negative.

- Remind me pain is only temporary, after five hours I may want to give up don't let me.

- Songs cheer me up.

- If I look like I am struggling don't panic, just keep shouting positive things to me.

- Please only be sick on the opposite side of the boat from me [If you have to be].

If I miss my tides do not let me give up and do not tell me. Just keep encouraging me.

• I may look blue and shiver, remind me to keep moving this is ok, I have worked through this before.

• Remind me not to touch the boat, if I do this I will be disqualified.

• The feeding list I have put together is not exhaustive.

Please use your discretion if I run out of things or anything gets spoiled.

• If I am sick in the water do not pull me out.

• Encourage me to carry on.

• Do not tell me if anyone is unwell on the boat.

• If a wave knocks me under, do not panic. Allow me time to surface and recover.

• Apparently many people give up an hour from France. Do not let me.

• If I say I will give up, do not let me. Talk me round.

• Remind me to deep breathe if I panic.

WHATEVER HAPPENS DO NOT LET ME EXIT THE WATER. "IT IS ALL IN THE MIND". REMIND ME OF THIS EVEN IF I AM IN EXTREME PAIN!!!

Failure is not an option! Keep positive for me!!

Whilst in Canterbury, I had to buy the rest of my supplies – I had drafted a big list. This was to be three swimming caps, three goggles, glow sticks, pasta, tuna, onions, blueberries, an extra swimming costume, six jars of goose fat, Ribena, baby food the banana variety, bananas, fruit juice, twenty mars bars, five flasks, plastic containers and jelly beans. My mumma had bought me a bag of the best jelly beans she could find in addition to the ones I bought. I felt a little like Jack in "Jack and the Beanstalk" as my jelly beans multiplied. When she handed them to me, a good feeling came over me.

My Mumma was very sweet; she drove me around wherever I needed to be. On the Monday, we had a call from the pilot telling us that the weather was very bad and stormy. My swim may be cancelled if the two swimmers before me needed to set off on a different day. I explained that whatever happened, I needed to swim on the 23rd, which was a Friday. A lot depended on this because this was the only day my crew could all be together. Also in the back of my mind, I had visualized the day and date for nine months now. Two and three together for me came to five and Friday was the fifth day and also the day I was born. Throughout the preceding nine months, every now and then, I kept finding five pence pieces and everything seemed to follow with the number five. I couldn't tell anyone this but it had to be this way.

My Mumma took me to Dover to watch the ships set off and we had hot chocolate to drink as the weather was stormy and the sea looked unforgiving that day. She gave me the option not to go ahead as we sat by the sea. I sighed and thought but I knew there was no way I was going to opt out.

The next day, whilst staying at my sister's, I told my family that I was going to go and practice swimming in

Dover and train there before my Channel swim. I could feel my chest still wasn't right but didn't want anyone to know this. I drove my Mumma's car to Dover. I sat on the pebbles and breathed in the sea air. I placed my hand in the water to feel the coldness of it as I watched the massive ferries leave dock and the massive container ships leave and go to sea. I shut my eyes at this point and visualized myself entering the water and reaching France. I did this for about an hour.

After the hour passed, I got up and then went back to my sister Bina's house. She is a very good cook and she made us lamb curry that night. For the rest of the week I stayed at my uncle's house off and on as well as my sister's. I was always looking at the weather, hoping my strength would be up for my swim.

I managed to get most of the items on the list although there was one thing I had not tested yet whilst I trained. I discovered that I needed a drink called Maxim. I had read a few articles on Channel swimmers that swore by it. It is a carbohydrate loader for athletes, to boost carbohydrate levels before exercise. Channel swimmers use it so they can consume enough carbohydrates to swim across the Channel. It was estimated that to swim across, a swimmer would expend more than eight thousand calories.

My Mumma and I had met the boatman and his son in Folkestone that morning and they had advised me that most people give up through pain. The tides were explained to me. I was told that I would not swim a straight line – it was more of an S shape and I would have to cross over the shipping Channel as well. The Channel from England to France was 22 miles but because the tide pushes you off course, it usually ends up being many more miles. I was happy to meet the pilot – he was smiley and grey. He was a real bear of a man, just what you would expect a fisherman to be. His son who worked with him on the boat was greying but thinner and smaller with a kindly face. The boat was pointed out to me. It was a small Rowenna fishing boat. I was very happy because it had FE75 on the side. Five has always been my favourite number on account of being the youngest of five and my parents both being one of five. My Mumma liked the boatman and told me she felt safer listening to them. She felt at ease and knew they would look after me.

A few days had passed but I was still struggling to get the Maxim, so my niece Poppy offered to go with me into town again and help me find what I needed. My Mumma drove us into Canterbury again and we searched for sports shops. I entered one sports shop and it was a little busy so I waited my turn and asked the shop assistant for Maxim, I said. "I am going on a long distance swim and was wondering if you could tell me if you have Maxim?" At this point while the assistant tried to sell me something else, a small thin lady interrupted. "Excuse me, I can help you. Please step outside." I did so. She introduced herself as a Russian Channel swimmer her name was Annika. "Are you looking to swim the Channel?" she asked. I nodded and said. "Well, hoping I can."

The information Annika imparted to me was brilliant! She told me of her failed attempt to swim the Channel and then of a successful relay team swim she did and that she regularly trains in the hope to swim it again solo next time. She said. "The first thing you need is Ibuprofen as you will be in a lot of pain because you will be injured. Get non-sleepy painkillers. Secondly, you're going to be sick, so buy mint tea and honey to soothe your throat because it will get infected. Also before you sleep, eat a lot of pasta and then wake up early. Drink lots and lots of water. Completely empty your body and bowels because many people fail due to stomach cramps."

I was astonished and automatically followed her. She had a sparkle about her with her quiet assurance and I wasn't about to ignore someone who wanted to give me good advice. Annika led me to the health shop that had the Maxim. I shook her hand, thanking her and we went our separate ways. I asked the lady in the shop for the Maxim and she said she didn't know of the product and that they didn't have it. I was crestfallen so I bought a similar product that she recommended.

When Poppy and I left the shop, Annika came rushing towards us. "Did you get it?" she asked. I explained that the lady didn't know anything about it. "Come with me." she said and we followed her into the shop. The shop assistant knew Anneka and she asked for the Maxim. She said, "You know you have some out the back." The assistant went at Annika's request and fetched the Maxim I needed. The best part was the product she fetched back was twenty pounds cheaper. Annika sorted out my refund. When we left the shop, we swapped numbers and she told me not to ignore her advice. I have to admit I had already made a mental note to get the items she told me about. We shook hands and I ended up giving her a big hug and waved goodbye. "Wow!" Poppy said. "She was really nice. It was really strange how she found us like that though Rowie." "I think someone is looking out for me Pops." I smiled and felt a good shiver down my back.

I spent the afternoon getting all my food made and packed making sure I added Annika's extra ingredients into the mix. My Mumma helped me make the pasta. I told her that I wanted it plain with no salt at all. My mum being the feisty matriarch she is, disagreed and said, "No, it needs salt and more flavourings." My uncle Ralph took me aside and explained I had to let my mum help me and I wasn't to argue because she needed to have some control. He told me that when I am in the water she would struggle.

The night before my swim, my cousin Venita, who was going to be a crew member was unwell but her fiancé was still ready to be a member of crew. My cousin Paul couldn't get leave from the army but luckily at the last minute, my friend Lucinda messaged me and explained that she would come over after work. This shocked me because she was scared of waves and water. So my crew consisted of Poppy, Isaac, Lucinda and my Uncle Mike as well as the pilot Peter and his son.

Uncle Ralph had arranged for some of my crew to stay at his pub the night before the swim. Isaac and my niece Poppy (Robina's daughter) would sleep at my sister's house and meet us the next morning at his pub so we could all set out together on the morning of the swim. My Mumma had me eat three plates of pasta and as my wish was to have a small whiskey, I duly got one. After my last meal, I was put to bed early. That was the hardest part because some of my family members were downstairs and I really did not want to miss out on any good conversations. Also, my friend Lucinda had not arrived yet. It was strange in a nice way – I felt like a small child again, being told what to do. My Mumma ushered me to bed and I crashed out until 3am.

Chapter Eleven

Day of the Swim

At 3am I woke up and to my surprise, my Mumma was up and waiting for me in the kitchen ready to make my breakfast. She made me toast and while I put my flasks of food and drinks together, she made me my first Maxim with hot chocolate. I was dying for a coffee so I had one small one. I drank many pints of water to flush out my system completely until it was time to drive to Folkestone from where I would start my swim.

It was still dark when my Mumma and I packed our car, filling the boot and back seat with all my foods, flasks, as well as blankets, warm clothing, etc., for my return crossing. It seemed like she had packed the whole linen cupboard and my complete wardrobe. I had so many things that Uncle Mike and Lucinda went in Uncle Mike's 4 x 4 jeep with their supplies. Uncle Mike and Lucinda, Poppy and Isaac all had to be dressed very warmly as they would be exposed to the cold sea air in the unsheltered boat whilst I swam. They had to take their food supplies to last them the duration of my swim and for the return journey. Isaac and Poppy had driven to Folkestone from my sister's house. I was told to rest while my crew unpacked the cars and I watched as the moon sparkled on the sea which slowly entered the docks.

My crew loaded a rowing boat four times with all the supplies and then took them to the seventeen foot fishing boat. The docks were so quiet – it felt very surreal. The day had come for me to swim the ocean. My Mumma was upset and I could tell this but she wasn't wanting me to know. She took my mate Lucinda aside and spoke to her and asked her to text, keeping her informed whenever she could. She told Poppy to switch off her iPhone and keep an eye on me at all times, not to be texting, etc. I hugged my Mumma many times before I walked to the rowing boat. She looked tearful as she said to me. "Don't you become a Mermaid in the sea, make sure you come back to me." She paused and then said "Otherwise we will both be mermaids in the sea," I smiled and hugged her.

It was hard for me to go in the rowing boat and leave my Mumma as she was alone that dark morning and I was not sure if she would know the way back to my uncle's pub, having never been to this harbour before on her own. We have always used my satnav. I climbed in and was rowed away to the fishing boat. I waved and waved because my mum waved and waved. I felt like jumping out and giving up so she wouldn't be upset. All these months I had trained, it dawned on me that I never considered my mum's fear of the sea. She was clearly now scared for me and I could sense it. Everyone had full battery charge and Lucinda and Uncle Mike were instructed to text my Mumma with any updates.

I climbed the ladder to get on the fishing boat and my Mumma was on her own at the docks just waving. This made me very sad because I knew she was scared and it had dawned on me that I had been selfish not to address this with her. She had always asked me about my plans and what needed to be done. She never once said "I don't want you to go".

My Pa hadn't been very well so he was in Portugal throughout everything. I felt some relief that my uncle and sister would look after my Mumma. My mum stayed at the railings until the boat set off and she waved until she was a small dot in the distance. I waved too and felt a tremendous sadness. At that point I wondered, dramatically, would this be my last day? I had read the worst stories of swimming the Channel as well as the best.

Chapter Twelve

The Swim

We set off from Folkestone harbour at 5.30am on Friday the 23rd of September. I had chosen my crew because they had the strongest stomachs that I knew of and I was warned that everyone would be sea sick whilst on the boat during their journey on my swim. Four people pulled out after I told them they were guaranteed to be sick and that they will be on a small fishing boat with no shelter for over sixteen hours. I was told grease up. My Mumma had instructed Lucinda and Poppy to help me smear grease on every inch of me, so they donned the plastic gloves she supplied them with and helped me apply three jars of goose fat all over me and my swimming costume. I had put the goose fat in the fridge the night before so we managed to apply thick layers on my body. It was almost impossible to put my goggles on – they slipped off each time I put them on. It took two people to place them on for me.

When I was eight hundred metres from Samphire Hoe, Peter the pilot said, "You can jump in now." This threw me because we had discussed the scenario and we had agreed that I would be rowed onto the beach and start from the shore. Peter said it was quicker for me to do it this way. I took off my favourite necklace and gave it to Poppy to wear. It was rather dark and I was quite scared so I asked for the ladder to climb down. Due to being covered in goose fat, I was too slippery to use it so I said "Well, I guess it is too late to start being scared now" so I jumped off the boat. As I did this my goggles came loose and I had to tread water slightly to fix them. I was so very, very scared. The boat shone a search light on me and I swam to shore. I followed the light because at this time I couldn't even see the shore. I was told that I had to swim to Samphire Hoe, stand up on the dry part of the beach and raise my hands. Peter had told me that I had to wait until the searchlight was on me to do this. I was then to start my swim.

It was still pitch black so swimming to the shore and getting my bearings was very difficult because even though I followed the searchlight, my vision was very bad due to the goose fat that was on the lenses of my goggles. When I got to the shore, there was an eerie silence that made my stomach go very nervous so I didn't adjust my goggles. I just stood up waved, using both my arms so the pilot could see I intended to start, and off I swam. It was so difficult to sight the boat but I did manage to line myself up eventually.

At the start of the swim, you have to line yourself up to the pilot boat. I breathe on my right side when I swim, so the boat kept to my right and I had to swim ten feet away from it at all times. This worked out well because my support crew were able to communicate with me as I swam.

After half an hour into the swim, I wanted to give up – I didn't say this but in my head I was thinking "You stupid fool, what you are doing?" I had put my Uncle Mike in charge of my feeds with Isaac as his second in command. Lucinda and Poppy were to assist and help them when they could.

The sun began to rise while I had my first feed. Isaac shouted "Rowie look behind you" and I did. I saw the White Cliffs of Dover and the gorgeous sunrise reflecting on them and I felt like I was in another world. It was during my first feed that I realized that all the training I had done of feeding on my back was impossible because if I went on my back I would not see approaching waves, I would run the risk of being knocked into the boat. Also, if I fed on my back, I could lose my sense of direction. I had to tread water instead, using my left arm. Uncle Mike threw my water bottle to me and I drank the Maxim that was mixed with Ribena – it was slightly warm. The bottle was attached with a piece of string. I could not touch the boat or I would be disqualified. For the rest of my swimming, I had made up my mind that I would only look right to the boat and not ahead of me. My reasoning for this was because I did not want to see that there was no land ahead of me, as it would make my swim seem longer. If I just looked right to the boat on my breaths, then I could keep a good line up with my crew.

I was so cold! The goose fat didn't really help – after an hour I was freezing. I knew swimmers put the goose fat on to stop the initial coldness of the water getting to them. To take my mind off the cold, I imagined being in a tropical country sunning myself, having coconut juice.

My feeds were every half an hour so I broke my swim into feeds to cope with the distance. Over the hours that followed I sang a few songs from The Kinks, White Stripes, Jimi Hendrix, The Stones, The Smiths, The Rolling Stones and a few songs from Vinyl Black Stilettos and Junksista.

When songs failed me because the cold took its grip, I thought back of Pa needing to be in Tenerife because it made me laugh at how many times he had got himself into bother. I thought about my sisters and Mumma all picking me up on different days from nursery in Mumma's blue VW Beetle.

I had told my crew not to tell me the time at any point and I didn't want to know how far I had swum. My game plan was just to keep swimming but at times, when the cold hit me, I feared hypothermia and the risk of hyperventilating because of the shock of the coldness. So I remembered being at my Granny's church and how I had to slow my breathing down. I was conscious of the fact that I had to keep relaxed in the water.

Uncle Mike kept my feeds to every half hour. The feeds were my resting point in that my body would get hydrated and fed. I couldn't physically rest because if I touched the boat once, I would be disqualified. Treading water whilst being fed was hard because my crew had a pole with a cup at the end of it in which my food was cut up and placed. I would then take the cup, have my feed and then they would give me my drink in a plastic bottle. This method was used throughout my swim. The waves would sometimes off balance me and I had to keep my legs powering just to stay in position. My crew managed to keep the feeds to less than a minute each time.

During the swim, there was one point where I felt something cling around my neck and my arms. I had decided to keep my eyes shut whilst swimming so my natural reaction was to think of the most dramatic outcome like a sea monster or a giant jellyfish. As you can imagine, I screamed in shock but to my relief my crew shouted to me that it was only seaweed. They then spent some time giggling at me while I unwrapped myself from the clutches of the seaweed.

Even though I wasn't looking at the land behind, in front or to the side of me, I did notice the weather and its changes. I began to get slightly less cold as the sun hit its highest point and I was grateful for the beams that hit my skin. It felt like it was only for a few moments and didn't last long before the cold came to me again.

My next feed was a little scary. I saw a massive black object block my whole horizon. I shouted in shock, "WHAT IS IT?" My goggles had grease on them so I didn't have a clear vision and just as I asked what it was, some big waves came and hit me and my boat moved up and down quite wildly. I was told that we were now in the shipping lanes and it was an oil tanker. I had to give way to the tanker because it would easily run us over. We had some rougher waves through the shipping Channel and in the back of my head, I remember the flasks I had bought. One flask had a glass interior and the others had steel. I became worried that my food may get ruined by broken glass if the flasks got knocked over. When I asked for the baby food on my next feed, I was told that it had been in the flask that had the glass interior and did smash during the rough waves onto the deck of the boat. I did not know at the time but my Uncle Mike replaced my food with his own that he had brought for the journey on the boat.

The tuna pasta that my Mumma put salt in I could not eat because each time I attempted to eat it, salty sea water made it even saltier. Whenever I had a feed it would invariably be mixed with sea water because of the splashing waves. However, I learned later that my crew ate the lot with relish.

The sun quickly began dropping in the sky and I found myself remembering many things, good and bad. It was like I had some sort of epiphany while I was in the ocean. I realized that life will always be full of twists and turns, pains and sorrows but it´s how we view life that matters. I realized that throughout my life, I have always had good, pure people who have loved me. Love had many forms and I had allowed myself to get caught up in romantic love. I had forgotten about platonic, matriarchal, paternal and pure love. I realized that every mistake I make in my life shouldn't be forgotten. Instead, I needed to learn that with each disappointment, I would become stronger and wiser.

One wave hit me and I swallowed too much water – this resulted in me being sick twice in the sea. I hated salty water and I knew from training that even if I had been sick, I would need to continue to swim. I was given honey and warm water to settle my stomach. Each drink had to be almost just tepid just so my body would not go into shock from extremes in temperatures.

I kept swimming and, just as the sun started to set, I felt extreme pain in both my legs. The cramp was agonizing. I lost my speed and the boat went ahead of me. Suddenly I heard Isaac's thunderous voice shout at me. "Rowie come on! Rowie come on!" I was briefly on my back through pain but then I remembered the time I got hypothermia in Caswell Bay in Swansea from stopping briefly. So I gritted my teeth and used my arms to power up in line with the boat. On my next feed, I drank all my water. I realized being sick had caused me to become slightly dehydrated and I had probably lost salt, which caused my muscles to seize up. My legs eventually started working again and I kept swimming.

Before the sun set completely, I saw something jump over me and I shouted. It happened two more times while I was having my feed. It turned out that three fishes had jumped over me. It reminded me of the grey finned thing that jumped out in the sea in Swansea and I smiled to myself. I saw it as a blessing because I was now starting to struggle and feel pain whilst swimming.

I found that the night came very quickly and my left shoulder started to become very painful. I took a painkiller and tried to swim through it. I realized that I would have to now concentrate more on my breathing... 1, 2, 3 breathe. 1, 2, 3 breathe. By focusing on breathing and slowing it down, I knew I could control my pain. At this point it was very strange, I smelled my Granny. She always used Ponds Cold Cream and that is exactly what I smelled. It gave me some comfort!

The darkness meant my crew ran the risk of losing sight of me so they had to give me glow sticks to put on. I tied these on to my goggles and swimming costume. My crew tied glow sticks to their wrists. At this point when I was swimming, I felt like I was in the sea just on my own. (And indeed I was all alone in the big wide ocean). The boat was all lit up but apart from the boat and me, it felt like nothing else existed. I felt a sudden respect for nature overcome me. I realized that I, as a human being, was just a small speckle in the vast universe that exists. Each time I took my breath, I saw the stars light the sky and because we were nowhere near land, there was no light pollution so everything reflected beautifully on to the sea.

The pain in my left arm became much worse and I found my right arm was guiding me forward and my left arm was really just keeping me afloat – it began to only do a doggy paddle type stroke. On my next feed I took another painkiller – this was to be my last one. I had taken two painkillers before my swim started as Annika had suggested and I wasn't to go over six because that would overdose me.

The darkness scared me as a child and even as an adult, I have always feared being in the dark so now I found myself facing extreme pain and one of my worst fears. At one point while I struggled, I felt something brush or knock my ribs. It was slight and I was too numb to scream or shout. In my mind I told myself it must have been debris. I didn't want to be taken out of the water so I made sure I didn't complain about the pain or the thing that brushed against me. My swimming time must have slowed considerably. Without the pull of my left arm I found myself veering towards the boat, which would have been game over for me had I touched it. I felt tiredness take its grip and my throat felt like I had swallowed a thousand knives. My feeds became harder to swallow and I found the warm drinks helped me if only for just the brief moments as it soothed my throat.

As time went on, I could see the night sky fill with the orange glow that comes with cities. I knew from the failed reports I read of swimmers, that many thought they only had an hour to swim after seeing France. In actual fact, I knew those lights meant I would have to swim at least another six hours before I even managed to get near the coast. I felt every wave hit me and push me back. I knew in the back of my mind, the eleven hours' completion time I had estimated, would be very far off due to my injured left arm.

Memories of my sisters taking me out on day trips as a child came into my mind and I held on to all the good memories to push me through my pain. I knew my fifty-five stroke per minute was now very slow and off pace. My swimming had no rhythm but still I carried on. As the pain got worse, I became disorientated and had less control of my body in the water. This is when I sensed my crew shouting at me. A wave hit me and I came dangerously close to hitting the side of the boat. Poppy was shouting. "LEFT "LEFT! LEFT! LEFT! LEFT!" I wasn't used to Poppy shouting. Throughout the swim, I knew she always kept her eyes on me and from the start she never stopped talking to me, telling me to keep going and keep swimming! The urgency in her voice woke me from the trance I had gone into and I used all my might to get my left arm out of the water. I used all my strength to correct my stroke and keep away from the boat. My crew came together like some huge glow stick monster and I was reminded of the rowers I used to see practice in Swansea as a child. My team shouted in unison. "Left! Left! Left! Left! Left! Left!" The glow stick monster that was multi-coloured waved me away from the boat. I remembered my mother's words. "You can rest when you're dead." My father's words "No such word as can't." I remembered every positive person that touched my life and I clung to those happy memories.

The pain in my arm was shooting down my neck and back. My ribs were in pain where something brushed against me and my throat was on fire…

I never really liked pop music. My sisters were all very alternative with their tastes as teenagers and they always tried to educate me. However my Mumma loved music in all its forms and was very eclectic with her taste. She brought us up with Motown, Ska, Reggae, Country Music, Classical music and music from nearly every era and genre. This one time I was moping around feeling sorry for myself, my Mumma had the music channel on television and called me to her. "Rowie look at this." she said, " listen to the lyrics Rowie, you should be singing this to that woman" (she called my ex this, not to be mean but even the

mention of my ex's name wounded me back then).
Beyoncé was on the TV and she sang:

"You must not know 'bout me
You must not know 'bout me
I will have another you by tomorrow
So don't you ever for a second get to thinkin'
You're irreplaceable (irreplaceable)..."

The bit of the song that came to me in the pain wasn't
the verse, it was the next bit:

"To the left, to the left.
To the left, to the left.
Mmmmm
To the left, to the left.
Everything you own in the box to the left"

I knew Poppy loved this song and just as I remembered
my Mumma showing me the song, my crew, the big multi-
coloured glow stick monster, all started to sing songs. To
keep me away from the boat they sang:

"To the left, to the left.
To the left, to the left.
Mmmmm
To the left, to the left.
Everything you own in the box to the left"

They sang Beatles' songs. The one I heard the loudest
was:

"We all live in a yellow submarine."

My crew danced and sang. They cheered me up
massively.

In the breaks, when I couldn't hear them singing, I kept thinking I was somewhere warm to fight the biting cold that was now taking over my body. To combat the pain in my throat, I imagined the best Scottish whiskey that I could, trickling down my throat. To combat my arm pain, well, there was nothing that could help with that. My memories of happy times and stories couldn't take away the searing pain – my arm refused to work, even the doggy paddle was now useless. I felt like I was swimming in mud.

I started shouting to myself in my mind:

"EASY! EASY! EEEAAAAAAAASSSSSY. EASY! EASY! JUST KEEP SWIMMING…"

"OOOOHHH I WANT TO DANCE WITH SOMEBODY."

"WOOOO TAKE ME DOWN TO PARADISE CITY…"
"PRINCE CHARMIN' PRINCE CHARMIN'"
"EAAAAAAASSSSSSYY EASSSSSY!!"

"Yeah, you really got me now
You got me so I don't know what I'm doin' now
Oh yeah, you really got me now
You got me so I can't sleep at night
You really got me
You really got me
You really got me"
EAAAAASSSSSY!

I went through all my old mix tapes in my head. I sang songs that I loved as an adult from bands like OIVA VOI, The Kinks and Ben Howard. Each time the pain got too much I shouted, "EAAAAAASY EASY." Suddenly a huge grey thing jumped in the sea behind me. It looked like what

I can only describe as a whale. I shouted and screamed. My trance was broken... I was quickly reassured that it was the boat´s dingy and that the pilot and my uncle were going to row ahead of me. The grease on the lenses of my goggles made it seem far more sinister than a dinghy.

I was told there would be no more feeds and I had to follow their flashlight. I hadn't practiced this part and it threw me because it meant I had to change my swimming to looking ahead. That was something that now was a very painful prospect as I had to adjust the way I was swimming. My crew sang one last rendition of "We All Live in a Yellow Submarine" and then the big glow stick monster waved me goodbye.

The grey dinghy was now a dot in my vision and I was following a flashlight that looked very much like a firefly.

My Uncle Mike shouted to me each time I drifted away from the light. "Rowie, this way. Rowie, this way." I struggled with the pain of adjusting my body to swim differently after what seemed like forever, it was far too much.

Jimi Hendrix was now my internal playlist and I got myself in a trance to keep my breathing secure and slow so that I would not panic and hyperventilate like I did at my Granny's church. That memory of Paul asking for an ambulance and being told Jesus would save me, made me smile and the coldness that was taking hold of my slowing body ebbed away briefly.

The moon looked very vain in the water as I swam with my head above the sea; the crescent shimmered and gave light to the sea. The stars gave me more light. The fishing boat that was brightly lit disappeared from my sight. The firefly I followed flickered and danced across the water.

I suddenly found myself parallel with the dinghy. "Rowie we can't come with you now. You need to go to shore on your own now and we can't follow. Remember you have to stand up and put your hands above your head to fully complete. The searchlight will hit you and once you are spotted you will have completed your swim. You will then need to swim back to us."

My mind was a fog of pain and delirious thoughts of whiskey and chocolate cake. I just mumbled, "Okay thank you" and continued swimming. The waves were gently lapping the shores and I left the dinghy's company to swim with the waves to the shore. Once again the firefly danced ahead of me and I followed. It seemed like many hours to do this. My pain was unrelenting.

When I got to the shore I smiled and in my thoughts I said, "Aah, standing will be easy." I was brought in by a gentle wave and my tummy hit the sand. I tried putting my legs on the ground to stand up. I found to my horror that my legs were total jelly. I thought. "Okay. This is to be expected. I will rest on the sand and look for a pebble while my legs wake up."

I couldn't find a pebble. I really wanted a French pebble to take back home. I decided I would try to stand. I tried one leg and before I could get my other leg into a crouching position, I fell flat on my face.

I took a deep breath and got to a half standing position but my legs gave way again. My body wanted to give up – the pain was too intense.

I tried a third time and I managed to stand up and just as I raised my arms, I fell down again from my own body weight and I felt all the pain surge through me.

For my fourth attempt I decided to chant to myself:

"Easy! Easy! EAAAAASSSSY."

I stood up and gritted my teeth and with tremendous pain, I lifted my arms up. The light in the distance flicked and flickered but it hadn't shone on me yet... My left arm was giving way through pain... I saw the spotlight and it hit me again. But this time... I heard a shout:

"Rowie you have completed it. Swim back."

Peter the pilot was shouting. He had some sort of megaphone.

Chapter 13

Sangatte, France

The beach at Sangatte, France was silent and I felt it had its own personality. The darkness, and not knowing what was on the beach with me, scared me. I had visions of all sorts of things coming after me. I was near to delusional with my imagination.

I looked to the sky and I saw the moon was such a lovely crescent shape and the stars twinkled. A smile came to my face and I felt a little safer in front of such majestic beauty. I realised that possibilities are endless and dreams do become a reality because here I was in France. I had swum all the way from England to France.

Anything was possible!

I dropped to my knees and crawled back into the sea. I let the water carry me and, with great pain, I swam through the waves that blocked me and wanted me to stay on the beach. I gritted my teeth to get back into the deep water and when I got to the dinghy, I had zero strength to haul my own weight into it. My uncle and the pilot lifted me over and they rowed me to the fishing boat. "Well done Rowie." My Uncle Mike said softly. "Now I have strict orders from your mum telling me that when you get back on to the boat I was to apply sun cream on your face. So, no arguments Miss Sunshine." I smiled at my Uncle and when we got to the boat my crew helped bring me aboard as I struggled to climb the ladder.

My crew was very sweet and cheered me on when I got on the boat. I felt warm by the love and thoughtfulness they showered on me. My response to their cheering was not so quick as I numb – the whole situation felt unreal at the time.

When I had asked everyone to be on my crew, I had not considered how they would feel mentally and emotionally watching me swim, etc. I later learned of how deeply affected they were as they watched me struggle during the last six hours of my swim because of the injury to my arm.

I was made a chocolate drink – it was a tepid temperature so that I would not go into shock and my crew covered me slowly in six different layers to keep me warm and preserve my heat. My Uncle had been given sun cream by my Mumma before the swim to put on my face so he put it on gently.

I was told that my swim took me seventeen hours and ten minutes. I started the swim at 6.15 am and finished at 23.25 pm. I smiled to myself because five has always been a special number to me.

Chapter 14

The Return Journey To Folkestone

The boat trip home was surreal. Our journey back to Folkestone consisted of my crew who all had their chairs in a circle around me.

I watched the ships trawling the waters with their nets and the sea seemed to me to have so many textures, almost like an oil painting from the reflections of the lights on the sea. I was told the shipping lanes were four miles in width. Apparently I ended up swimming about thirty-six miles because I got pushed off course so my S shape was a lot bigger and I was lucky to catch the coast.

We all tried to stay awake but no sooner had one of us nodded off than another followed – it started a dominoes affect.

My Uncle Mike looked very pale as he tidied up all our equipment and food containers, etc., and at the same time checking that I was ok. He had quietly gone and put himself to sleep under the rowing boat that was propped up at the side of the deck so he was sheltered from the elements. It was a very cold September morn. I noticed my niece Poppy was very sleepy but she got up from her chair and put a blanket over Uncle Mike. He looked so vulnerable, thin and small as he lay there sleeping.

Although I was in pain and in shock from now completing my swim, I soon realised just what sacrifices my crew had made to come onto the boat to support me. When I saw Poppy making sure Uncle Mike was warm I felt overwhelmed. She was the youngest of my crew and yet there she was having compassion to her Great Uncle. I wondered how my crew coped. I knew that being on the boat was far colder than being in the sea because they had no physical activity to keep them warm as well as the fact that the sea is warmer than land. To be constantly on watch and having my life in their hands couldn't have been an easy task. I felt a great admiration for my crew as I watched them all doze off on their chairs. At last they could relax.

When we finally arrived at the English coast in Folkestone, it was about 3am so I thought my Mumma would be asleep and I would see her later at my uncle's pub. The pilot rowed us to shore and my crew took what was left of my supplies back to the shore. As I hobbled with my niece and crew to the cars, my Mumma suddenly appeared, screaming with excitement. She took me by the hand and shouted: "Woooooooo! Hup! One! Two! Three! Hup! One! Two! Three!" She skipped me to the car. Don't ask me how I skipped. I felt great joy and shock from seeing her appear from nowhere. It felt more like a hobble but my Mumma's excitement gave me great warmth.

As we got to the cars, loads of familiar faces jumped from behind parked cars screaming and shouting and cheering. Over thirty members of my family hugged me nearly all at once! I nearly had a heart attack with the shock of it all. My mum produced a massive bottle of pink champagne out of nowhere. I got so excited, I shook it up and sprayed everybody with it. My cousins and my Uncle

John and Aunty Gem had all turned up to greet me. It was so heart-warming to have such love around me. I felt like a new chapter had started in my life and no matter what I went through from now on, I could face anything.

We had a party at my Uncle's pub and when I got in the bath later, the pain I felt where something had hit my ribs, had become a massive bruise down my side. I was cut to bits under my arms and neck. My whole body was in agony but I couldn't be happier.

My family made me goat curry and my wish of a good whiskey came true. I was honoured with the finest whiskey the pub had. That liquid gold was a tonic for my ripped throat. My Uncle Ralph opened a magnum of champagne that he had given to him years before by his son at his son's wedding and would not even open on his sixtieth birthday. He also had a microphone ready encouraging me to make a speech. I did a short speech gave the microphone to my Uncle Mike who must have been exhausted but still did his bit. He then and passed the microphone on to Uncle Ralph who did a brief speech. He then gave the mike to my Mumma and encouraged anyone who wanted to speak. My brother-in-law Chris made a very touching speech, followed by Venita, I was humbled with everything they all had to say. However, I was slightly embarrassed by all the attention I seemed to be getting.

I was later told by my Uncle Ralph that my Mumma was quiet for the duration of my swim, apart from when she gave him updates of my progress. She stayed in her bedroom and didn't talk throughout the day. He said it was the quietest he had ever known her in all his life. It was only when my Aunty Gem came toward the end of my swim that my Mumma opened her door and spoke. I felt a little sad hearing that my mumma was so scared for me.

I reflected on my nine months and realized that I had everything to live for. It dawned on me that when I needed rescuing, family and friends gathered round me and filled me with unconditional love.

THE END

"The path of life is mixed with twists and turns...

When you are up it brings you down...

When you're sure your path is right it trips you off it...

What remains constant is love from friends and family...

Gain strength from positive people and thoughts...

When your body feels broken and your mind follows...

Seek lessons that strengthen the soul and heal the mind...

Giving up is never the option. Get up...fall down...
Make sure you heave yourself back up time and time again.

Out of all uncertainty, love...pure love brings us through.

Honour your friends and family and never shut your soul to the beauty of the natural world because it knows you...

Never ever give up.

Don't work so very hard and believe you can rest when you die.
Those years will go swiftly when you live out of balance...
Your best friends will become strangers.
Your family will become distant.

Working too hard and never living will crush your soul
Centre yourself and each day make time for those that
matter.
Don't put your work before your family.
Trust me when I say your company will not put you
first.
Instead wake each morning and plan your life...
Take in the wonder of nature...
Work smarter not harder...
Make time for your friends even if you're tired...
That painting you always wanted to paint... turn the TV
off and paint

Those dreams you have... Strive to make them a reality
You may think that without working hard you can't
give your family what they want.
Trust me... Your time is worth so much more...
Take your family for long walks and homemade
picnics...
Learn to make things as a family...
Take each day as a new blessing don't become
complacent...
The pain in your heart when time has flown by leaves
you the question of... What If?
Here's the thing... live and love...
Share and laugh...
Dance and play...
Live in balance...